SUMMER SCENES
COLORING BOOK

Teresa Goodridge

DOVER PUBLICATIONS, INC.
MINEOLA, NEW YORK

Over thirty beautifully detailed scenes in this book are sure to make the experienced colorist feel bright and sunny. Use colored pencils, markers, or even watercolors to bring the beach, a fair, a relaxing afternoon in a bountiful garden, or a romantic wedding, among other designs, to life. Best of all, the pages are perforated for easy removal so you can display your finished work.

Copyright
Copyright © 2016 by Dover Publications, Inc.
All rights reserved.

Bibliographical Note
Summer Scenes Coloring Book is a new work,
first published by Dover Publications, Inc., in 2016.

International Standard Book Number
ISBN-13: 978-0-486-80933-5
ISBN: 0-486-80933-1

Manufactured in the United States by RR Donnelley
80933101   2016
www.doverpublications.com

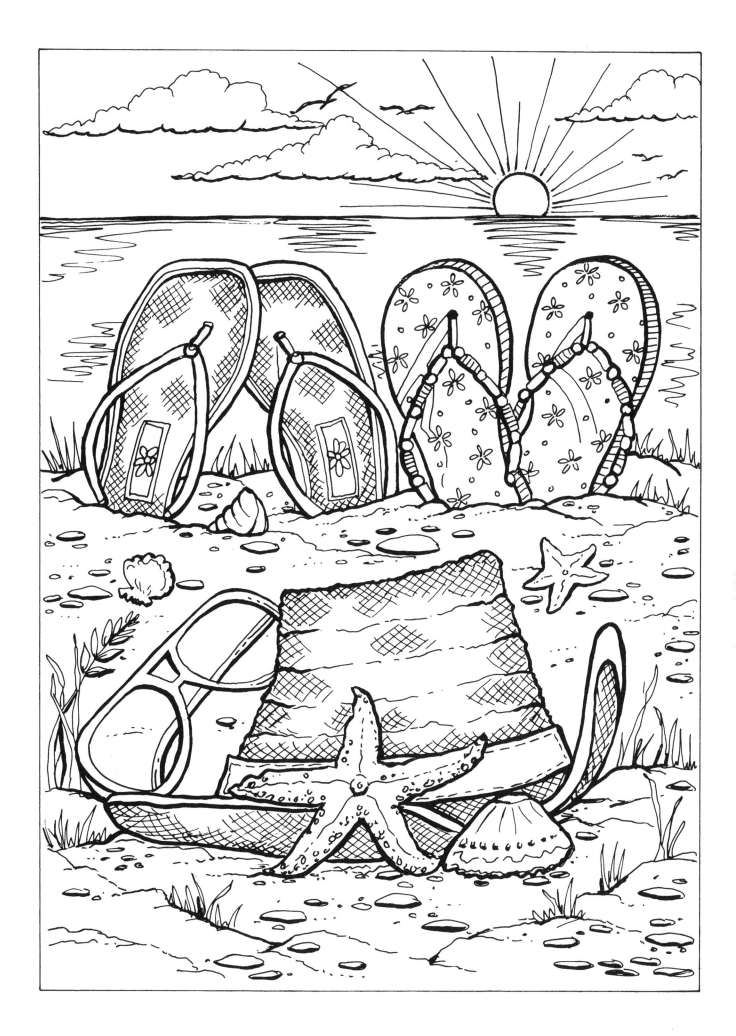